Cooking

Gill Tanner and Tim Wood

Photographs by Maggie Murray
Illustrations by Mark Peppé

A & C Black · London

Here are some of the people you will meet in this book.

The Miller Family in 1990

The Grant Family in 1960

Tony Miller is the same age as you.
His sister, Jane, is eight years old.
What is Tony's mum called?

This is Tony's mum, Helen,
when she was nine years old, in 1960.
She is with her mum and dad,
her brother and her baby sister.

The Brown Family in 1930

The Jennings Family in 1900

This is Tony's granny, Rose, when she was just a baby, in 1930. Her brother, John, is looking after her.

This is Tony's great grandma, Victoria, when she was six years old, in 1900. Can you see what her brothers and her sister are called?

Can you spot the differences between these two kitchens?

One is a modern kitchen and one is a kitchen a hundred years ago.

This book is about kitchens and cooking.

It will help you to find out how these have changed in the last one hundred years.

There are eleven mystery objects in this book and you can find out what they are.
They will tell you a lot about people in the past.

Anna Jennings used this in her kitchen
a hundred years ago.
It is about as tall as this book.
Can you guess what it was for?
If you turned the handle,
what do you think would happen?
Turn the page to find out.

Can you find the mystery object in this picture?
It's an **egg whisk**.
Anna Jennings turned the handle of the egg whisk to mix the eggs and flour together.
Anna made all her own cakes, puddings and bread.
Victoria helped her.

In those days, people couldn't buy many kinds of ready-made food in packets.
Does your favourite pudding come in a packet?

This mystery object is nearly as tall as you.
It was the most important thing in Anna Jennings' kitchen.
What do you think it is?

Here are three clues.
1 It got very hot.
2 It did three different jobs.
3 In your home, you have something like this, but smaller.

Turn the page to find out what it is.

Can you spot the mystery object?
It's called a **kitchen range**.
Do you have something like this at home?
What is it called?

You can see that the range was used for cooking.
The range also heated the house and it heated the water.
A hundred years ago, very few people had electricity
or gas for heating.

This mystery object is
a bit bigger than a chair.
Anna Jennings used it
near the kitchen range.
She mostly used it on Sundays
and at Christmas.

Look very closely.

Can you guess how it worked?

Have you ever seen
anything like it?

**Turn the page to
find out what it is.**

The mystery object is called a **Dutch oven**.
Anna Jennings used it to roast a big piece of meat.

1 She hung the meat on hooks.

2 She put the Dutch oven in front of the range.

3 She wound up the clockwork motor. The motor turned the meat round, so it cooked on all sides.

4 She opened the door to see if the meat was cooked. Is there something like this in your kitchen?

This mystery object is about the same size as the egg whisk.
It comes from Victoria Brown's kitchen.
What do you think she used it for?
Look carefully, you may spot a big clue.
What is the hole in the top for?

Turn the page to find out.

This is Victoria Brown's kitchen in 1930.
How is it different from her mother's kitchen?
Can you spot the mystery object?
It's a **bean slicer.**

Victoria's mum cut the tops and tails off the beans.
Victoria put the beans in the slicer.
When she turned the handle, a sharp knife
on the side of the machine cut the beans into slices.
In those days, not many people had fridges.
Victoria bottled her beans to keep them from going mouldy.

Victoria Brown often used these both together.
The round object is about the same size as a saucepan.
What are these mystery objects made of?
How did Victoria use them?
Turn the page to find out.

Can you spot the mystery objects?
One is a **sieve** and the other is a **presser**. Which is which?

Victoria pressed cooked vegetables through the sieve, to make baby food for Rose.
In those days it was harder to buy baby food in tins and jars so lots of mothers made their own.

This mystery object is about the same size as a jug. Victoria Brown used it to make something which tasted really good. Can you spot a big clue which tells you what it was for? What happened when Victoria moved the handle?

Turn the page to find out.

Can you spot the mystery object?
It's a **cream maker**.
Victoria Brown put milk and melted butter in the cream maker.
When she moved the handle up and down, the milk and butter mixed together and turned into cream.

Victoria used the cream to decorate cakes and jellies when John or Emma had a party.

These mystery objects come from Rose and Peter Grant's kitchen. You can probably guess what they were used for. But do you know what they are made from?

Turn the page to find out.

This is the Grants' kitchen in 1960.
How is it different from the Browns' kitchen?
It was much easier to keep clean. Can you see why?

The mystery objects are a **jug** and a **bowl** made from **plastic**.
Plastic was a new material in those days.
It was light and could be washed easily.
The lids on the bowls and jugs
stopped the air from getting in,
so they kept food fresh for a long time.

This mystery object is as tall as you are.
There is something like this in your kitchen.
It is one of the most important things in the kitchen. Do you know why?
What happened when Rose Grant pulled the handle?

Turn the page to find the answer.

Can you spot the mystery object?
It's a **refrigerator**.
Refrigerators keep food fresh for a long time.

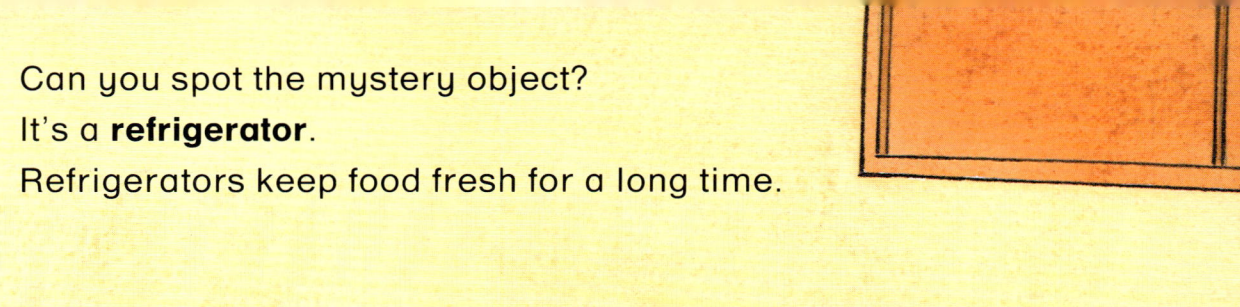

Rose Grant did her shopping in the supermarket.
She bought food for a whole week because
she knew it would stay fresh in her refrigerator.

She put frozen food, like peas, in the freezer.
Frozen food will keep fresh for months.
What else can you see in the refrigerator?

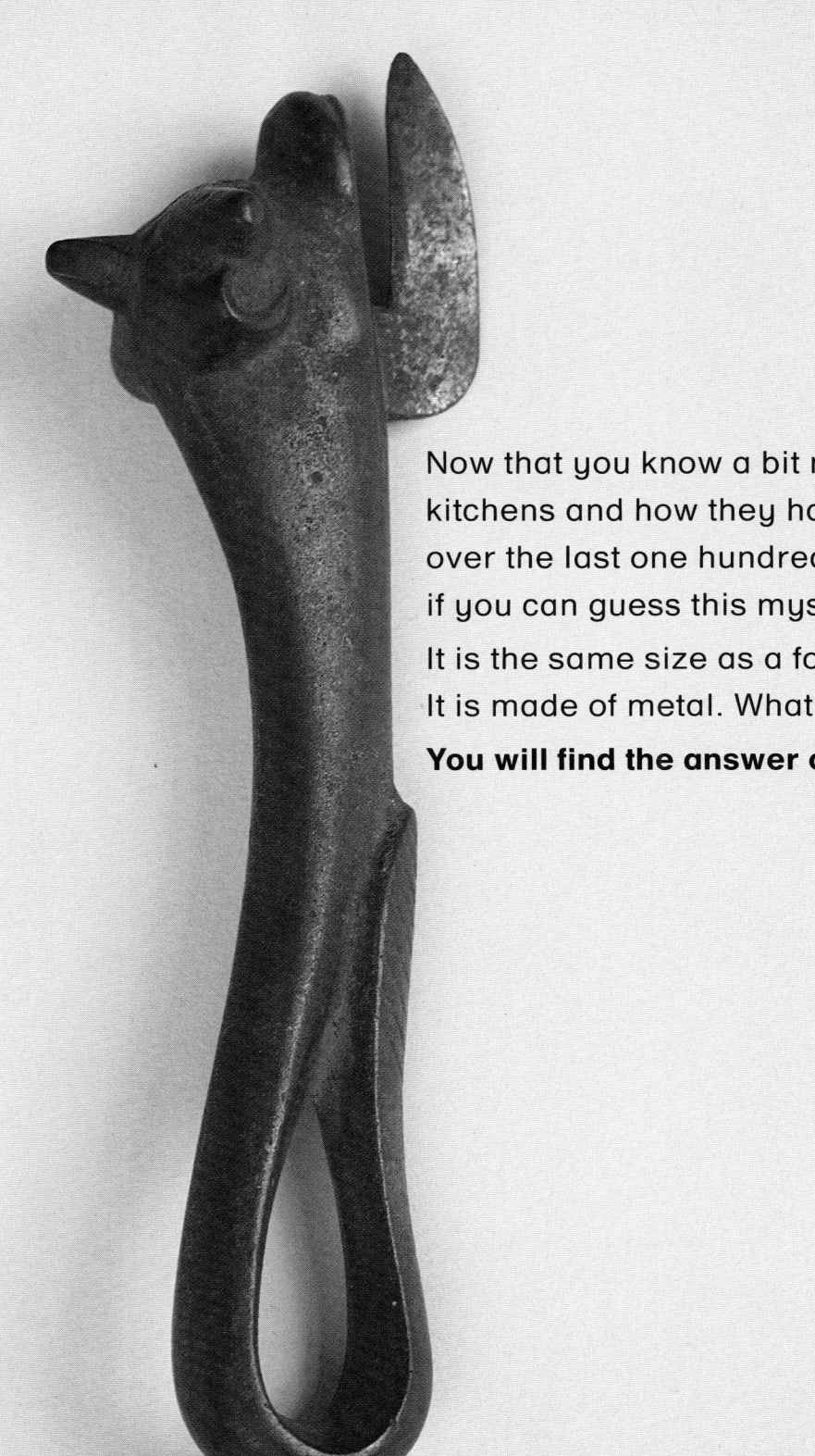

Now that you know a bit more about kitchens and how they have changed over the last one hundred years, see if you can guess this mystery object.

It is the same size as a fork.
It is made of metal. What is it?

You will find the answer on page 24.

Time-line

These pages show you the objects in this book and the objects we use for cooking nowadays.

PREPARING FOOD

1900
The Jennings family

egg whisk

1930
The Brown family

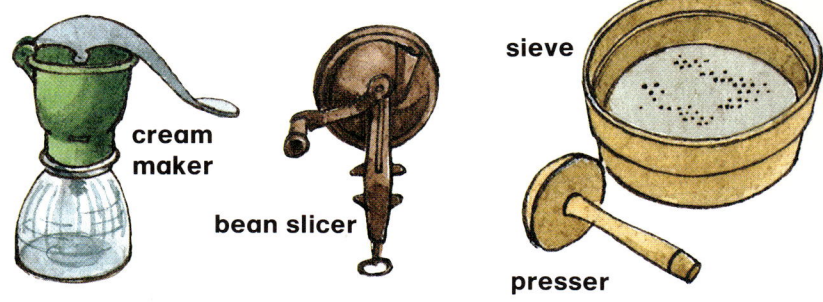
cream maker

bean slicer

sieve

presser

1960
The Grant family

1990
The Miller family

food mixer

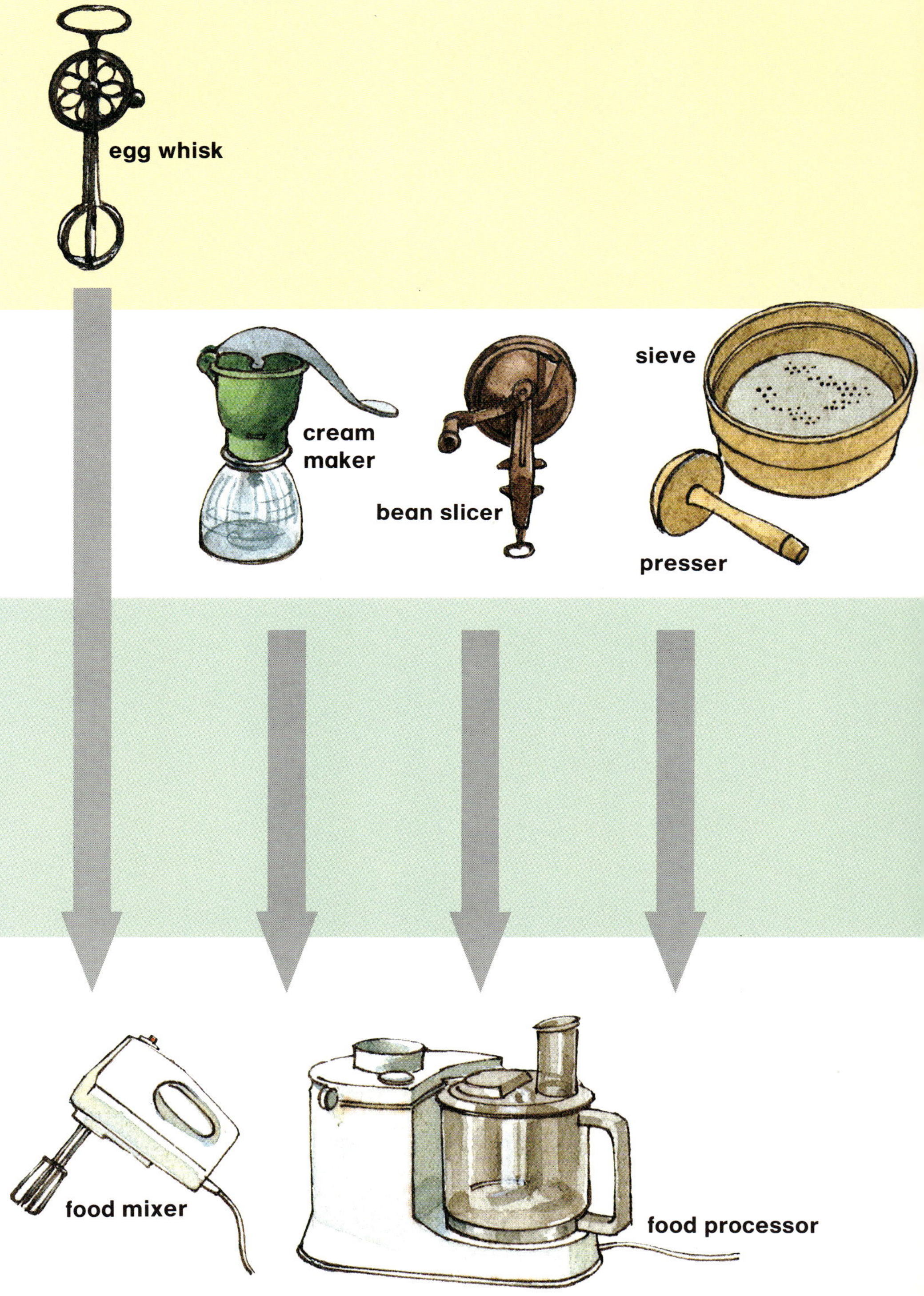

food processor

COOKING FOOD

STORING FOOD

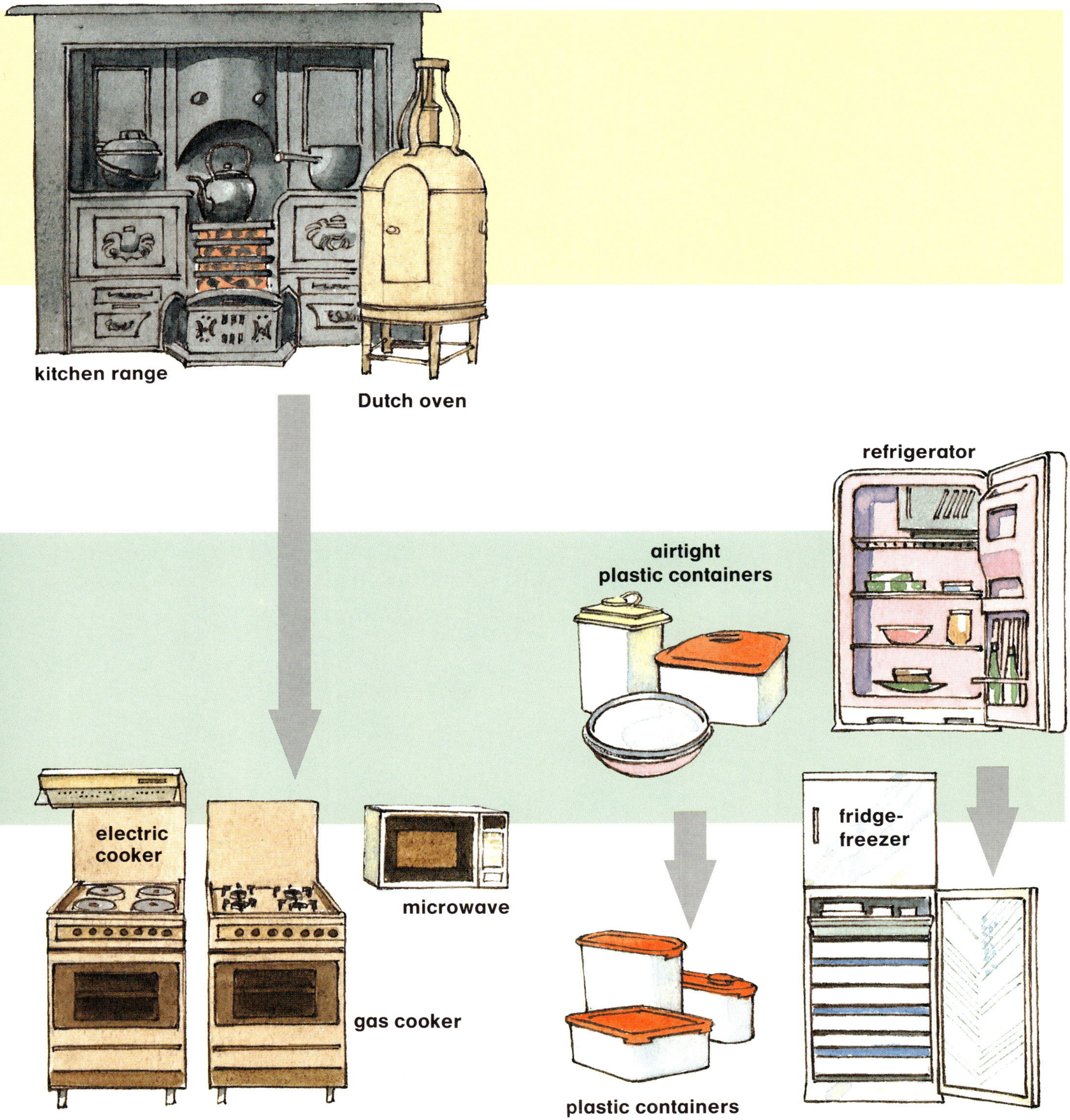

kitchen range

Dutch oven

airtight plastic containers

refrigerator

electric cooker

microwave

gas cooker

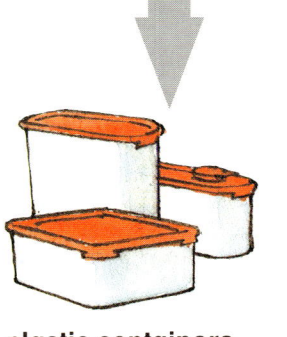

plastic containers

fridge-freezer

Index

Bb baby food *14*
bean slicer *11, 12, 22*
bottling *12*
Browns' kitchen *12, 13, 14, 15, 16*
Cc cakes *6, 16*
cream maker *15, 16, 22*
Dd Dutch oven *9, 10, 23*
Ee egg whisk *5, 6, 22*
electricity *8, 23*
Ff food processor *22*
frozen food *20*
Gg gas *8, 23*
Grants' kitchen *17, 18, 19*
Hh heating water *8*
Jj Jennings' kitchen *5, 6, 7, 8, 9, 10*
Kk kitchen range *7, 8, 9, 23*
Mm mouldy *12*
Pp packets *6*
plastic *18, 23*
presser *13, 14, 22*
puddings *6*
Rr ready-made food *6*
refrigerator *12, 19, 20, 23*
roast *10*
Ss sieve *13, 14, 22*
shopping *20*
Tt tins and jars *14*

The **mystery object** on page 21 is a **tin opener**. In 1900 this would have been given away with a tin of corned beef. To open the can, you pushed the pointed end into the tin and wiggled the handle up and down. It was very dangerous to use.

For parents and teachers

More about the objects and pictures in this book

Pages 5/6 The Jennings family lived in a large industrial town. Their kitchen had no electricity and no piped water. The egg whisk is almost identical to a modern one but not rustproof.

Pages 7/8 The kitchen range remained popular until after 1918 when electricity and gas started to reach more homes. It burned coal, wood, even household rubbish, and it was kept alight all the time.

Pages 9/10 This is the Victorian equivalent of the modern rotisserie.

Pages 11/12 The Browns lived in a semi-detached house in a small town. Prices of fresh food varied through the seasons so salting and pickling were common. Notice the gas cooker, running water and electric light; also the new 'wipe down' surfaces.

Pages 13/14 In the 1930s, the absence of refrigerators in most homes forced many mothers to make their own baby foods.

Pages 15/16 In the 1930s, few shops had refrigerated display cabinets so, in towns, fresh cream was hard to buy.

Pages 17/18 The Grants lived in one of the new towns built in the 1960s. In the 1960s people started making weekly shopping expeditions to the supermarket by car. The first household objects made of polythene were washing-up basins which were manufactured in 1948. Tupperware was introduced to Britain in the 1950s.

Pages 19/20 Before the invention of the domestic refrigerator, housewives stored their food in meat safes. These were either insect-proof cabinets kept in a shady place outside the house, or small cabinets made of some absorbent material, such as pottery, with a water reservoir on the top. The evaporation of the water cooled the cabinet. The first domestic refrigerator was sold in Britain in 1924. The first frozen foods in Britain were made in 1939.

Things to do

History Mysteries will provide an excellent starting point for all kinds of history work. There are a lot of general ideas which can be drawn out of the pictures, particularly in relation to the way houses, clothes, family size and lifestyles have changed in the last 100 years. Below are some starting points and ideas for follow up activities:

1 Work on families and family trees can be developed from the family on pages 2/3, bearing in mind that many children do not come from two-parent, nuclear families. Why do the people in the book have different surnames even though they are related? How have their clothes and hair styles changed over time?

2 Find out more about cooking in the past from a variety of sources, including interviews with older people in the community, magazines, books and manufacturers' information. People of different social class and from different areas ate very different foods.

3 There is one object which is in the 1900s, 1930s and 1960s kitchens. Can you find it?

4 Experiment to find the most effective ways to stop food from going bad, and the most hygienic materials for kitchens.

5 Look at the difference between the photographs and illustrations in this book. What different things can they tell you?

6 Make your own collection of cooking objects or pictures. You can build up an archive or school museum over several years by encouraging children to bring in old objects, collecting unwanted items from parents, collecting from junk shops and jumble sales. You may also be able to borrow handling collections from your local museum or library service.

7 Encouraging the children to look at the objects is a useful start, but they will get more out of this if you organise some practical activities which help to develop their powers of observation. These might include drawing the objects, describing an object to another child who must then pick out the object from the collection, or writing descriptions of the objects for labels or for catalogue cards.

8 Encourage the children to answer questions. What do the objects look and feel like? What are they made of? What were they used for? Who made them? What makes them work? How old are they? How could you find out more about them? Do they do the jobs they are supposed to do?

9 What do the objects tell us about the people who used them? Children might do some writing, drawing or role play, imagining themselves as the owners of different objects.

10 Children might find a mystery object in their own kitchen for others to draw, write about and identify.

11 If you have an exhibition, try pairing old objects with their nearest modern counterparts. Talk about each pair. Some useful questions might be: How can you tell which is older? Which objects have changed most over time? Why? What do you think of the older objects? What would people have thought of them when they were new? Can you test how well the objects work? Is the modern version better than the older version?

12 Make a time-line using your objects. You might find the time-line at the back of this book useful. You could include pictures in your time-line and other markers to help the children gain a sense of chronology. Use your time-line to bring out the elements of *change* (eg. the gradual development of gas and electricity, the development of labour saving gadgets and cleaners, more streamlined kitchens) and of *continuity* (eg. basic similarities in the processes of cooking, and the need for hygiene, heat, light and water).

History Mysteries

First published 1992
A & C Black (Publishers) Limited
35 Bedford Row, London WC1R 4JH

ISBN 0–7136–3491-X

© 1992 A & C Black (Publishers) Limited

A CIP catalogue record of this book is available from the British Library.

Acknowledgements

The authors and publisher would like to thank Suella Postles and the staff of Brewhouse Yard Museum (Nottingham), Mrs Tanner's Tangible History, Hilary Gawel and Jane Baxter, Lucy, Nick, Kate and Stella, and Flashback for the use of their 1960s fridge.

Apart from any fair dealing for the purposes of research or private study, or criticism or review, as permitted under the Copyright, Designs and Patents Act, 1988, this publication may be reproduced, stored or transmitted, in any form or by any means, only with the prior permission in writing of the publishers, or in the case of reprographic reproduction in accordance with the terms of licences issued by the Copyright Licensing Agency. Inquiries concerning reproduction outside those terms should be sent to the publishers at the above named address.

Filmset by August Filmsetting, Haydock, St Helens
Printed and bound in Italy by L.E.G.O.